Runaway Bike!!!

Sam and Oliver walked slowly down Sutherland
Avenue with Murray, their pet duck.

"Look out!" Oliver heard someone scream.
"Runaway bike!"

Oliver spun around and saw Rusty Jackson
barreling straight at them. "Look out!" Rusty
screamed. "Out of control!" He had a mad look
in his eyes as his bicycle zoomed down the
sidewalk.

"He's trying to run us down!" Sam yelled.
"Get out of the way!"

OLIVER
AND
THE
LUCKY
DUCK

OLIVER AND THE LUCKY DUCK

PAGE McBRIER

Illustrated by Blanche Sims

Troll Associates

Library of Congress Cataloging in Publication Data

McBrier, Page.
    Oliver and the lucky duck.

    Summary: Oliver takes in a wild duck with a broken
wing and hopes to keep it as a pet after it has healed.
    1. Children's stories, American. [1. Ducks—Fiction.
2. Pets—Fiction] I. Sims, Blanche, ill. II. Title.
PZ7.M47830l   1986   [Fic]   85-8417
ISBN 0-8167-0541-0 (lib. bdg.)
ISBN 0-8167-0542-9 (pbk.)

CHAPTER 1

Oliver Moffitt sat on his bed, counting his profits.

"Not bad," he said to himself. Since starting his own pet-care service, Oliver had at last been able to save almost enough money for a new, deluxe pet-grooming kit.

He scooped up the coins and bills and stuck them back into a mayonnaise jar. "One more good customer and I'll have what I need," he said. Oliver took the first two volumes of *Caring for Your Pet* off his bookshelf and hid the jar behind the books again.

He was the only kid he knew who had his own business. Dog-walking and cat-sitting were his specialties, but of course Oliver knew much more than that. In fact, he liked to think that he knew just about everything there was to know about pets.

Up until this month, business had been booming. Oliver had cared for dogs, cats, birds, and even two goldfish named Goldie and Locks. But the phone hadn't rung for a month now.

"Maybe it's time for a new advertising campaign," Oliver thought. The phone on his desk rang.

"Oliver Moffitt's pet-care service," he said.

"Hi, it's Sam." Samantha Lawrence was Oliver's next-door neighbor and classmate. "What are you doing?" she asked.

"Nothing," Oliver replied.

"Want to go for a bike ride in the park?" she asked.

"I really should be here in case customers call," said Oliver.

"What if we take some of your flyers to the park and pass them out?" said Sam.

Oliver's face brightened. "I'll meet you outside in five minutes," he said.

Mrs. Moffitt's dog, Pom-pom, came running into the room. "Want to go for a bike ride?" Oliver asked. Pom-pom was a Shih Tzu, a toy breed from China. Mrs. Moffitt spoiled him rotten. Pom-pom yapped happily and wagged his tail. He loved to ride in Oliver's bike basket.

Downstairs, Mrs. Moffitt was bent over her desk in the living room, paying bills.

Oliver's parents were divorced, and he and his mother had lived alone for as long as Oliver could remember. He hadn't seen his father since he was a baby.

"Hi, Mom. I'm taking Pom-pom for a ride in the park," Oliver said.

"What a good idea," said Mrs. Moffitt with a smile. "It's a beautiful spring day."

Five minutes later, Oliver and Sam were pedaling up Sutherland Avenue. " '*I'm a little acorn brown, I'm forever falling down,*' " sang Sam. She knew just about every camp song that had ever been written. They turned the corner and headed into Arrowhead Park.

As they rode past the baseball diamond, Oliver saw his friends Matthew Farley and Josh Burns. "Hi, guys," he said. "Getting ready for Little League?"

Josh nodded and put down his glove. "Where are you going?" he asked.

"To pass out flyers," Oliver replied.

"Want to come?" asked Sam.

Josh and Matthew ran over to their bikes.

"We were tired of practicing anyway," said Matthew.

The foursome pedaled past the ball park.

"Want to go visit the ducks first?" Oliver said. "I haven't been to the pond since I took care of Princess Fluffy."

"Sure," said Sam. "Too bad we didn't bring any bread with us."

When Oliver was little, the duck pond was his favorite spot. As they approached the pond, Oliver could see lots of grownups holding small children by the hand.

Pom-pom stood up in the basket and wagged his tail.

"Let's go over to the other side, away from all the little kids," Oliver said. "Pom-pom likes to chase the ducks away and eat their bread crumbs."

They parked their bicycles next to a big, shady tree and walked to the edge of the pond.

"Sure is quiet on this side," Sam said.

"It's kind of creepy," Matthew whispered.

Josh looked at Oliver and rolled his eyes. Matthew was such a chicken.

Pom-pom disappeared behind a clump of bushes. "He's either trying to sniff out leftover bread crumbs or frogs," Oliver said.

A loud commotion came from the bushes. Oliver could hear Pom-pom's excited bark.

"What's that funny noise?" said Sam.

Oliver sighed. "He probably saw a frog."

"I think we should investigate," said Josh.

"It's only a frog," Oliver repeated. He looked over and saw the bush shake violently. "Maybe you're right," he said.

Pom-pom was still yapping.

"Quiet," Oliver demanded. Everyone peered into the tangled bush.

"Look!" cried Sam. "It's a stuck duck."

Oliver pushed the branches aside. "It looks like he's hurt," he said.

They took a closer look. The duck was wedged between several thorny-looking branches. One of its wings was bent in the wrong direction.

"Gross," said Matthew.

"Help me get it out," Oliver said. As Sam and Josh held the branches back, Oliver gave a

gentle tug and freed the bird. It lifted its head weakly and dropped back, exhausted, on Oliver's arm.

"The poor thing," said Sam. "It must have been stuck in there for days."

"I think its wing is broken," said Oliver. "See how it sticks out funny?" The bird gave a feeble quack. Pom-pom looked at the duck and whimpered.

"We have to get it to the vet right away," said Sam. She took off her jacket and wrapped it around the duck. "I can carry it in my bike basket."

Oliver picked up Pom-pom and ran over to his bike. "Are you coming?" he asked Matthew and Josh.

"Can't," said Josh. "We're having company for dinner."

Matthew fidgeted and looked at the ground. "I think I should be going, too," he said. "I'm not too good around hurt animals."

The Animal Emergency Center was close by. Oliver had been there once before when Pom-pom ate a whole box of chocolates (including part of the box) and had to have his stomach pumped.

"Dr. Johnson, please," said Oliver to the receptionist. "Tell him Oliver Moffitt is here." Oliver looked over at Sam. "He's their best vet."

Oliver leafed through a copy of *Today's Vet* while Sam quietly sang campfire songs to the duck. Oliver and Sam were the only ones in the waiting room.

Suddenly the front door opened again. A huge Labrador retriever barreled into the room. Oliver looked up from his magazine just as the dog noticed the duck. The dog froze. It slowly lifted its right front paw off the ground. Its nose quivered.

Oliver saw the duck pick up its head uneasily. "Stand on the bench, Sam," he hissed. Sam quickly obeyed.

"Leave the duck alone, Chief," said the dog's owner. "We're not hunting today." The man explained to Oliver, "He points at the ducks when I go shooting."

For a minute it looked like a stand-off. Then, from underneath the bench, Pom-pom charged the Labrador.

"Pom-pom! Are you crazy?" Oliver shouted.

Pom-pom nipped ferociously at the big dog's paws, but Chief only looked confused.

"Stop trying to be a hero," said Oliver. "That dog will tear you apart."

Pom-pom ran underneath the dog's stomach, still barking.

"Watch out!" yelled Sam. But it was too late. The big dog sat down.

Pom-pom let out a shriek. Oliver could see the tiny dog's head peeking out from underneath Chief's stomach.

"You're squishing Pom-pom!" Oliver shouted. The Lab didn't move.

"Get up, Chief," said the dog's owner.

Chief yawned and looked the other way.

"Let me handle this," said Oliver. "I'm very

good with dogs." He walked over and grabbed Chief's collar. Chief snarled.

"I'll give him a few minutes," Oliver said quickly.

Pom-pom tried to wiggle out. Chief looked at him and growled.

"Do something," Oliver told the dog's owner. "My dog can't breathe under there."

The man shook his head. "Chief is pretty set in his ways," he said. "I don't like to cross him."

Pom-pom had managed to get one paw free and was waving it in the air.

From the direction of the bench, Oliver heard a peculiar sound. "What's that hissing noise?" he asked.

Sam and the duck were still standing on the bench, but the duck had suddenly revived itself. Its head began to bob back and forth like a snake's.

"*Sssssss*," said the duck. Its eyes flashed angrily at Chief.

Sam stood very still. "I think he's upset," she said.

Chief looked at the duck and whined. Without another sound, he stood up and walked over to the front door, his tail tucked between his legs.

Pom-pom hopped up and shook himself. He ran behind Oliver and growled ferociously at Chief again.

"Stop that," Oliver said.

"Why don't we wait outside?" said Chief's

owner. "I can see that your pets don't get along with Chief." They both disappeared quickly.

Sam sat down on the bench again. Pom-pom jumped up on Oliver's lap and nuzzled the duck. The duck gave a low, contented quack.

"Look at that," said Sam. "They like each other already."

Dr. Johnson came out to the reception area. He was wearing a long white coat. "Hello, Mr. Moffitt," he said with a smile. "How's business?"

"A little slow," Oliver replied. Pom-pom ran over to the doctor and wagged his tail.

"Hello, Pom-pom," said Dr. Johnson. "Are you staying out of trouble?" Oliver was glad Dr. Johnson hadn't shown up a few minutes earlier. He pointed to Sam, who was still cradling the duck in her arms.

"We found this duck at the duck pond," said Oliver. "I think its wing is broken."

Dr. Johnson examined the duck carefully. "You're right," he said. "Fortunately it looks like a pretty clean break."

"Can it be set?" asked Oliver.

"Certainly," replied the doctor. "We can insert a pin through the wing that will hold it in place until it heals."

"How long will that take?" asked Oliver.

"About four weeks," said the vet.

Oliver thought for a minute. "It would be better if we kept the duck at home while he's healing, right?"

Dr. Johnson frowned. "Keeping a wild bird is illegal in this state," he said. "But you can't really set the bone, let him go back to the duck pond, and expect the wing to heal properly. He's too weak. He needs someone to look after him for a while."

"I understand," said Oliver. He looked at Sam. "I don't know how Mom is going to take this," he said. "Dogs and cats are one thing, but—"

"Oliver," interrupted Sam, "don't forget that I found him, too. We're both responsible for him. Besides, it's only until he gets better."

"Mom shouldn't mind if it's only for a month," Oliver said. He looked at Dr. Johnson. "Let's set the wing."

Dr. Johnson smiled. "Fine," he said. "One more thing. Because of your pet-care business, I can give you a professional discount. But you're still going to have a pretty hefty bill. Do you think you can handle it?"

Oliver thought about all the money he had saved in his mayonnaise jar. Then he looked over at the duck, who gave him a sad quack. "No problem," Oliver told the doctor. "My business will pay for it."

Sam, Oliver, and Pom-pom waited patiently while Dr. Johnson set the wing. Chief and his owner were still outside. When Dr. Johnson came out of the examining room, Sam and Oliver rushed over.

"All done," said the doctor with a smile. "With a little tender loving care, your duck should be up and quacking in no time."

"Great!" said Sam

"Any special instructions?" asked Oliver.

"Do you have a fenced-in yard?" asked Dr.

17

Johnson. Oliver nodded. "Good," said the vet. "How about a children's wading pool for the duck to bathe in?"

"I think my old one is still in the garage," Oliver replied.

"What about shelter?" asked Sam.

"He should be all right this time of year if you have some nice, shady trees," said the doctor. "Better yet, you can build a small house. Just make sure it has a dry floor, good ventilation, and a nice, wide door. Ducks hate to squeeze through narrow openings."

"What do we feed it?" asked Oliver.

"You can pick up duck pellets and cracked corn at the pet store." Dr. Johnson wrote out a prescription. "This is for vitamin drops to put into his drinking water. Be sure you also pick up some grit."

Sam made a face. "What's grit?" she asked.

"It's very fine gravel," Oliver explained. "Birds use it to help them digest their food. It goes to their gizzards and helps act as teeth."

Dr. Johnson smiled. "I'm sure this little fellow will get well soon with such experts looking after him."

He went back inside and came out holding the duck in his arms.

"Aw, look," said Sam "He's wearing a sling."

"You can leave that on for the first few days until he gets used to the pin," said Dr. Johnson. "Other than that, he just needs lots of peace and quiet."

Oliver gently stroked the duck's downy white head. "What should we call you?" he said.

"I know!" said Sam. "Let's call him Murray. I have an Uncle Murray who looks just like him."

Oliver thought for a moment. "How about it?" he asked the duck.

Murray paddled his feet in the air.

"I think he likes it," said Oliver. "Let's take you home and introduce you to Mom."

CHAPTER
2

"**Y**ou found a *what*?" said Mrs. Moffitt. Oliver was trying to shout to her through the shower door.

"A duck," he said again. He stood in the hall with Sam, Pom-pom, and Murray.

Mrs. Moffitt shut off the water and poked her head out the door.

"Oh!" she said with a start.

"Mom, it's only a duck," said Oliver.

Mrs. Moffitt took a closer look. "Is that a sling?" she asked.

"He broke his wing. We rescued him," answered Sam.

"May we just keep him until he gets better?" said Oliver. "He'll stay in the back yard. I promise he'll be good."

Murray gave a convincing quack.

Mrs. Moffitt sighed. "Why couldn't I have

a son who was interested in computers or cars?"

"Then it's okay?" said Oliver.

His mother smiled.

"Yay!" shouted Sam. "C'mon, Oliver. We've got work to do."

In the back yard, Sam put Murray down. He grabbed several large bites of grass and headed for the gate.

"Oh, no, you don't," said Oliver, closing the fence.

Pom-pom strained at his leash.

"Maybe you should let them be together," said Sam.

Oliver undid Pom-pom's leash. Murray didn't look up from his eating. "Sorry, Pom-pom," Oliver said. "Murray is more interested in food."

After his meal, Murray walked the entire length of the yard. Pom-pom followed cautiously behind.

"I'm going to try to find that old wading pool," said Oliver. He headed for the garage.

"Look!" laughed Sam. "Murray and Pom-pom are following you."

Oliver turned around. "Quack, quack," said the duck as he tried to keep up with Oliver.

"I think he likes me," Oliver said. "Hey, here's the pool. Let's check it out."

That afternoon, Oliver and Sam made a special trip to the library. A book called *Ducks in Your Back Yard* contained lots of helpful information. "Look, Sam," Oliver whispered, "did you know that Murray is called a white Pekin? That's the kind of duck they use for eating."

"I wouldn't tell him that if I were you," said Sam with a grin. "You might give him the wrong idea."

"It says here that white Pekins aren't usually wild," Oliver said, looking up from the book. "Maybe Murray belonged to somebody and wandered away from home."

"I never heard about anyone around here keeping ducks," she said.

"Who knows where he could have come from?" Oliver said. "Murray might have flown hundreds of miles." They leafed through the book some more.

"Whoa," said Sam. "Look at this!"

"It's a diagram of a duck house!" said Oliver.

Sam examined the picture closely. "It looks pretty easy to make," she said.

"Are you sure?" Oliver asked. He didn't know the first thing when it came to building things.

"A piece of cake," Sam assured him. She closed the book and stood up. "Do you think you can get your mom to drive us to the lumber yard tomorrow?"

"Probably," Oliver replied.

"Perfect," said Sam. "It shouldn't take more than an afternoon to put this together."

When they returned to Oliver's house, Sam used a hose to fill the old wading pool. "That patch we put on the pool works," she said. "No water is coming out."

"Okay, Murray," Oliver called. "Time for a swim."

Murray saw the wading pool and came running.

"In you go," said Oliver. He lifted Murray up and plopped him into the pool.

Murray dipped his head under the water and then fluffed out his feathers.

Oliver took off his shoes and socks and stepped into the wading pool, too. "Aaaah," he said. He and Sam both laughed. "I think having a pet duck is going to be just great."

From inside the house came the sound of Pom-pom's impatient barking.

"Coming," Oliver yelled. He opened the kitchen door. Before Oliver could stop him, Pom-pom shot across the yard and jumped into the wading pool. Murray flapped his wings and hopped out.

"Bad dog," said Oliver. "You get out of there right now." Pom-pom's feet barely touched the bottom of the pool as he wagged his tail.

Murray looked at Pom-pom and made the same hissing sound he'd made at Dr. Johnson's office.

"Pom-pom, I'd get out of there if I were you," Oliver warned.

Pom-pom wagged his tail again and barked.

With an angry hiss, Murray leaned over and took a jab at Pom-pom's tail. Pom-pom gave a surprised shriek and jumped out of the pool.

"You see?" said Oliver. He picked up the

little dog. "You made Murray mad. And now you're too wet to take for a walk."

Murray hopped back into the pool.

That night at dinner, Pom-pom sat in the corner and refused to touch his meat loaf and mashed potatoes.

"That's strange," said Mrs. Moffitt. "I've never known him to turn down meat loaf."

Oliver didn't say anything.

Mrs. Moffitt buttered a small piece of bread. "See if Pom-pom would rather have this," she said.

Oliver took the bread over to the corner. "Here, Pom-pom," he said.

Pom-pom snarled. Oliver quickly pulled his hand away and sat back in his chair.

"Pom-pom!" Mrs. Moffitt exclaimed. "What's gotten into you?" She looked at Oliver. "Did something happen today that made Pom-pom unhappy?"

Oliver moved the mashed potatoes around on his plate.

"Did Pom-pom get a walk today?" Mrs. Moffitt said.

Oliver shook his head. "He fell into Murray's wading pool and was too wet to go outside," he said. He didn't want his mother to know that Murray had bitten Pom-pom's tail. Mrs. Moffitt would probably make Murray leave.

"Poor Pom-pom," said Mrs. Moffitt. "I suspect he's feeling a little neglected." Pom-pom looked at Mrs. Moffitt and whimpered.

"Faker," Oliver said under his breath. Pom-pom

would do anything for attention.

"Oliver," said Mrs. Moffitt, "I'd like to remind you that you do have a responsibility to Pom-pom. If you can't handle two pets around here, we'll just have to go back to having one."

"But Mom," Oliver protested, "I haven't neglected Pom-pom."

Pom-pom rolled over on his back and whined again.

"Please try a little harder," Mrs. Moffitt said.

Pom-pom walked over to his saucer of meat loaf and licked the plate clean.

The next day, Mrs. Moffitt drove Oliver and Sam to the lumber yard, where they bought wood, nails, screening, and a bag of sawdust for the duck-house floor. Oliver's mayonnaise jar was now empty.

"That wiped us out," he said with a sigh. "Where will we get the money to buy duck food?"

Sam pulled a few dollars out of her pocket. "I have some allowance money I can chip in."

Oliver pushed the money away. "I can't take your allowance," he said.

"No, really, it's okay," said Sam. "We agreed that we'd both be responsible for Murray, remember?"

Oliver took the money reluctantly. "Thanks," he said. "But that's it for allowance. We'll have to find another way to earn money, okay?"

"That's fine with me," Sam replied.

When they got home, Sam started right to work. "Do you have a saw?" she asked.

Oliver shook his head.

"Never mind," said Sam. "I'll get one from my house."

By dark, the duck house was nearly finished. Sam stood back to survey her handiwork. "Looks kind of like a fat doghouse," she said.

The duck house had a wide front door and a roof that slanted toward the back. Above the door were three screened windows. Inside, the floor was scattered with sawdust for warmth.

"Murray," called Oliver, "come see your new house."

Murray waddled over from the other side of the yard, where he and Pom-pom had been digging in the grass. He looked around, then quickly hopped inside.

Pom-pom tried to follow. "No, Pom-pom," said Oliver. "That's Murray's house." Pom-pom wagged his tail and jumped in anyway.

"I'm glad they're friends again," said Oliver.

The next day at school, Oliver and Sam's teacher, Ms. Callahan, invited them to the front of the room to talk about Murray. Sam drew a diagram of Murray's house on the blackboard and explained how they had built it. Ms. Callahan told the class that it takes a lot of math know-how to build a duck house.

After Sam and Oliver sat down, Ms. Callahan said, "The Science Fair is coming up soon.

Maybe Oliver and Sam can think of a way to use Murray."

Oliver sat next to Matthew at lunch.

"Murray sounds really neat," Matthew said. "I'm glad you're going to keep him. When can I come visit?" The only pet Matthew was allowed to keep was a bowlful of tetras. Fish were okay, but Oliver thought they got a little boring.

"How about after school?" Oliver said. "Sam has Girl Scouts today, so she's busy. After we visit Murray, you can help me take Pom-pom for his walk."

"Great!" said Matthew.

A paper airplane came flying across the cafeteria. It had been glued together with a blob of peanut butter and jelly.

"Gross," said Matthew.

Oliver stood up. He could see a bunch of older boys snickering in the corner. "I think it came from over there," he said.

Matthew picked up his tray. "Let's go out to recess," he said. As the two boys crossed the cafeteria, another paper airplane sailed by.

"That one just missed me," Oliver said. He looked over at the corner again.

"Looking for something?" said one of the boys. It was Rusty Jackson. Rusty was the meanest, sneakiest kid in school. He had once lost a bicycle race to Oliver and Pom-pom. Ever since, he'd been trying to get back at Oliver.

"What do you want?" asked Oliver.

Rusty casually folded together another paper

airplane. "Just wondering if you had anything planned for the Science Fair yet," he said.

"Maybe," said Oliver.

"I don't suppose you'd like to make a little bet?" said Rusty.

Matthew pulled on Oliver's arm.

"Like what?" said Oliver, shaking Matthew away.

"Like if I win the Fair, I get that stuffed owl," said Rusty. Oliver's stuffed owl was his most prized possession. He had received it for winning last year's Science Fair.

"I don't know," Oliver said.

"Chicken," said Rusty. His friends all snickered.

Oliver shook his head. He didn't even have an idea for a project yet. Still, he wasn't going to let Rusty make fun of him like that. "I'll think about it," he said.

Rusty laughed. "I'll be in touch, pal," he said. He stood up and shot another paper airplane across the room. It hit a little girl in the head. She started to cry.

"Good shot," said Jay Goodman, one of Rusty's friends. They all started to laugh again.

Oliver and Matthew turned to leave. "A total creep," Oliver said under his breath.

At three o'clock, Oliver and Matthew walked home together.

"Here he is," said Oliver. He unlatched the gate, and Murray quickly waddled over to them.

"Why don't you watch him while I get Pom-pom ready for his walk?"

When Oliver and Pom-pom returned a few minutes later, Murray was following Matthew around the yard.

"Do you think Murray wants to go on our walk with us?" said Matthew.

"I don't know," said Oliver. "He might run off."

"We can put a leash on him," Matthew suggested.

"Good idea," Oliver replied. "Wait here." He came back with Pom-pom's rhinestone leash. Oliver looped the leash around Murray's neck and gave a gentle tug. "Heel," he said. Murray obediently followed.

"This is fantastic!" Matthew exclaimed. "A duck on a leash. We should go somewhere."

"Let's go to the park," Oliver said.

Oliver and Murray got a lot of attention as they walked along Sutherland Avenue.

"Look, Mommy!" screamed a little girl. "A duck!"

Oliver smiled with pride. "Hello," he said.

Several cars slowed down as they passed.

"Good afternoon," said Matthew with a wave. Pom-pom barked and Murray quacked.

"Which way?" said Matthew when they got to the park.

"How about the rose garden?" said Oliver. "Until Murray gets better, we should keep him away from the little kids."

Soon they were sitting on a bench as Murray

rooted around under the rosebushes. "Murray, get out of there," Oliver said. He gave the leash a tug.

Murray squawked and tried to go in the other direction.

"Wait!" said Matthew. "He's got something shiny in his mouth." Matthew reached over and pulled it out. "Wow!" he said. "It's a gold watch. Someone must have lost it."

Oliver looked over Matthew's shoulder. "It's got diamonds on it, too! I bet it's worth a fortune."

Matthew turned the watch around, looking at it sparkle. "I wonder who it belongs to?"

Just then, Kimberly Williams and Jennifer Hayes walked up. They were both in Oliver's class. Jennifer was carrying a stack of record albums.

"Is this Murray?" asked Kim.

"Yes," said Oliver.

"Hello, little ducky," said Jennifer. She pretended to give Murray a kiss.

"Ducks don't like to be kissed, Jennifer," said Oliver.

"Look what Murray just found," said Matthew. He dangled the watch in front of Jennifer's nose.

"Wow! Let me see that!" she said.

Matthew snatched the watch back. "No. It's ours," he said.

"What are you going to do with it?" asked Kim.

"We're not sure," said Matthew.

"You could sell it for a lot of money," said Jennifer.

Matthew held out the watch again. "It even has diamonds," he said.

"It's really beautiful," said Jennifer. "I bet you could get a couple of thousand dollars for it."

"Lucky," sighed Kim.

Murray and Pom-pom continued to scratch around in the bushes.

Oliver thought for a minute. "I think we should report it to the police," he finally said. "After all, it isn't ours to sell."

"I guess not," said Matthew.

"Besides," Oliver continued, "Murray found it, not us."

Oliver looked at Kim and Jennifer. "Want to come with us?"

"Can I hold Murray's leash?" Jennifer asked.

"No fair," Matthew protested. "It's my turn next."

"You can watch Murray when we go inside the police station," Oliver told Jennifer and Kim. "We aren't supposed to keep a wild bird. It's illegal."

"Can I hold Murray's leash then?" said Jennifer.

"Okay," said Oliver with a sigh.

The police station was right on the edge of the park. Jennifer and Kim waited around the back of the building.

"We'll be out soon," Oliver said. He and Matthew walked inside and up to the front desk.

33

A sign on the desk said LIEUTENANT MILLER. Behind it sat a policewoman with her hair pulled in a bun. "Yes?" she said, looking at them.

Matthew started to fidget.

"We were walking in the park and we found this watch," Oliver said. He nudged Matthew, who pulled the watch out of his pocket.

"That's a valuable watch," she said.

"It's probably worth a couple of thousand dollars," Matthew said.

The woman laughed. "Maybe." She took out a piece of paper. "Why don't you tell me where you found it?"

"You mean no one has reported it missing yet?" said Oliver.

"Not yet."

The policewoman promised to give him a phone call if anyone claimed the watch. Oliver didn't mention Murray.

They went behind the station to find Jennifer and Kim carrying Murray and Pom-pom around like babies. "Did you find the owner?" asked Jennifer.

"Jennifer," said Oliver. "Please be careful. Murray just had his wing set. I don't want him getting hurt again."

"Okay, okay," she said. "We were playing doctor and nurse."

"No one came looking for the watch yet," Matthew said.

"I told you you should have sold it," said Jennifer. She gave Murray another kiss and set him back on the ground.

35

Oliver made a face. "Let's go home," he said to Matthew.

At dinner, Oliver told his mother about the watch.

"It sounds like you did the right thing," she said.

Oliver thought about the empty mayonnaise jar. "I probably could have gotten a couple of thousand dollars for that watch."

"It wasn't yours, was it?" said Mrs. Moffitt.

"No." Oliver sighed and got up to clear the table. On his way to the kitchen, he peeked out the window at the back yard. Murray had already gone to his duck house for the night. He'd finished all the apples and duck pellets in his dish.

Oliver sighed again. Ducks were expensive. On Wednesday he'd have to make another trip to Perkins' Pet Supply. The kitchen phone suddenly rang.

"Oliver, answer that, will you please?" said Mrs. Moffitt from the dining room.

Oliver picked up the phone.

"Moffitt residence, Oliver speaking," he said.

"Oliver, this is Lieutenant Miller from the Fifth Precinct. I spoke with you earlier today. I wanted to let you know that someone has claimed that watch you turned in."

"Really?" said Oliver.

"The owner would also like to give you a reward," said Lieutenant Miller. "She'd like you to have fifty dollars."

"You're kidding!" said Oliver. "Wow, that's great!"

"Then you accept?" the policewoman said.

"Fifty dollars is a lot of money," Oliver said. "It was no big deal to turn the watch in."

"What's going on?" Oliver's mother asked from the table.

"Just a minute, Mom," he answered.

"Oliver, I'm sure you could use the reward money for something," Lieutenant Miller said. "Don't you have a hobby or something special you're saving for?"

Oliver remembered Murray. After all, he was the one who found the watch. That fifty dollars would help pay for a lot of duck pellets. "Um, could you please hold on for a second?" he said.

Oliver put down the the phone and ran into the dining room. "Mom," he said, "someone claimed the watch. They want to give me a reward—fifty dollars. I can really use that money to pay Murray's expenses. What do you think?"

Mrs. Moffitt smiled. "I think that's a wonderful idea," she said. "Murray is certainly turning out to be a lucky duck."

Oliver went back to the phone. "Okay," he told Lieutenant Miller. "What do I have to do to get the reward?"

Before he went to bed that night, Oliver stepped outside to check on Murray. The duck was asleep.

Oliver was careful not to disturb him. He made sure the back-yard gate was latched securely, then quietly turned off the porch light. "Good night, Murray," he whispered.

CHAPTER
3

T he next day, Oliver could hardly wait to tell his friends about the reward.

"I would have used the money to buy more albums," said Jennifer.

"But we owe bills for Murray," Sam said.

"So?" said Jennifer. She laughed, and walked off to find Kim.

After school, Sam and Oliver rushed home. Murray seemed glad to see them.

"You think we can take him for another walk?" said Sam.

"Sure. Why not?" said Oliver. "The exercise is good for him." Oliver ran inside and returned with Pom-pom. "Just a short walk, though," he said. "We don't want to strain him. I took his sling off only this morning."

Sam and Oliver walked slowly down Sutherland Avenue.

"Look out!" Oliver heard someone scream. "Runaway bike!"

Oliver spun around and saw Rusty Jackson barreling straight at them. "Look out!" Rusty screamed again. "Out of control!" He had a mad look in his eyes as his bicycle zoomed down the sidewalk.

"He's trying to run us down!" Sam yelled. "Get out of the way!"

Oliver, Sam, and Pom-pom moved just in time. Murray let out a loud squawk and flew to the top of a tall wooden fence.

Just as he reached Oliver and Sam, Rusty swerved to the left and threw on his brakes. "Ha, ha, scared you," he said with a sickening grin.

"You idiot," said Oliver. "Now look what you've done." He pointed at the fence. "Murray is all the way up there. He's not supposed to do any flying until his wing is healed."

Rusty started to laugh. "You mean to tell me you have a pet *duck*?" he said. "First it was that sissy dog, and now this."

Pom-pom whimpered and crawled between Oliver's legs.

"Stop it, Rusty," said Sam. "You and your big jokes."

Rusty ran over to stand underneath the fence. "Quack, quack," he yelled up. "Quack, quack, quack."

Oliver had enough. "Now you're going to get it, Rusty," he said. He ran over to the fence, but Rusty was already climbing back on his bicycle.

"Cool down, sport," he said. "Can't you take a joke?"

"You'd better hope Murray isn't hurt," Oliver said, shaking his fist. Rusty laughed and rode off.

"Forget about him," said Sam. "I'm scared about Murray."

They both looked up at the fence. "Come on down, Murray," Oliver said. "It's safe now."

Murray didn't budge.

"I think we have to go get him," Sam said. "He doesn't look like he wants to move."

"I hope he's all right," said Oliver.

Sam stood on Oliver's shoulders and hoisted herself on top of the fence.

"I'll wait down here," Oliver said. Sam was the best athlete in class. He knew she could do the job.

"Fine," Sam shouted back. She was already climbing along the fence toward Murray.

"Don't worry, Murray," Oliver yelled. "Sam's coming to the rescue."

He watched Sam reach Murray. "Have you got him?" he called. "Careful, now. Watch out for that wing." Pom-pom looked up at the fence and whimpered.

Sam carefully tucked Murray under one arm, then handed the frightened duck to Oliver.

"Good work," said Oliver. He gently inspected Murray's wing. "Everything looks okay," he said. "What a relief. This duck sure is lucky."

"You're telling me," said Sam. She brushed

some dirt off her jeans. "Let's get him home before anything else happens."

On Wednesday, Sam, Oliver, and Josh sat in Oliver's yard watching Murray play in his pool.

"You know," said Sam, "I've been thinking about what Ms. Callahan said about using Murray for our Science Fair project. It seems that Murray has a lot of good luck. I bet if we entered him in the Science Fair, he'd be sure to win."

"You're right!" said Oliver. He thought about Rusty's bet. "What should we do?"

"I don't know," Sam replied. "Why don't we all think about it for a few days?" She looked over at Josh. "You too, Josh. You're supposed to be the class brain."

Josh grinned. "Okay," he said.

Sam stood up. "I've got to go now," she said. "Mom and Dad are wallpapering the bathroom tonight and I've got to help them."

After Sam left, Josh and Oliver watched Murray splash around some more.

"Why don't we go to the Quick Shoppe?" said Josh. "I'll treat you to a soda."

"Great," Oliver replied. "Let's take Murray with us. Pom-pom's already had a walk today."

Oliver let Josh hold Murray's leash all the way to the store. Josh had a small box of raisins left over from lunch. Every so often, he'd feed a few to Murray.

"Oliver," said Josh, "look how Murray loves

raisins. I bet we could use them to teach him a few tricks."

"That's not a bad idea," said Oliver. "Maybe we can rig something up for the Science Fair."

When they got to the Quick Shoppe, Murray tried to follow Josh inside.

"No, Murray," said Oliver. "We have to wait out here."

"Hello, young man," said someone behind Oliver. It was the Cat Lady. Her little red wagon, filled with cats and cat supplies, sat next to her.

"I haven't seen you in some time," she remarked. The Cat Lady fed all the stray cats in town. Once she had helped Oliver look for Jennifer's cat, Princess Fluffy, after Oliver had accidentally lost her.

Oliver tightened his grip on Murray's leash. Several of the cats looked at Murray and licked their chops.

"Hello," said Oliver. "I've been busy taking care of a duck."

"Ducks?" she said. "You've got ducks now?"

"Just one," Oliver replied. He pointed to Murray.

"Why do you want a duck? There are so many stray cats that need good homes."

"It's just for a little while," Oliver replied. "He broke his wing."

"What did he do that for?" the Cat Lady asked with a smile.

Oliver looked inside the Quick Shoppe for Josh. A big orange cat had climbed off the wagon

and was crouched underneath it. Oliver could see its tail twitching.

"Don't mind Mr. Chips," said the Cat Lady. "He won't hurt anyone."

Mr. Chips made a low, throaty snarl.

"Are you sure?" asked Oliver.

The Cat Lady pulled a cat snack out of a large paper bag. "Here, Chippy," she called. "Come to Mother."

Mr. Chips edged closer to Murray.

"Now, you stop that," said the Cat Lady. She reached down to pick up the cat.

Mr. Chips ballooned to twice his size. His fur was standing completely on end.

"I think we'll be going," Oliver said hurriedly.

It was too late. Mr. Chips charged.

"No!" screamed Oliver. "Get away!"

"Young man, don't hurt my cat," said the Cat Lady. "He doesn't mean any harm."

Murray took off across the parking lot with Mr. Chips hot on his heels.

Oliver caught up to Murray and stepped on his leash. "Gotcha!" he cried. He scooped Murray up in his arms and ran back toward the Quick Shoppe. Looking over his shoulder, he saw that Mr. Chips was still on his trail.

"Look out!" yelled a woman's voice.

Oliver turned around to see a woman with two full grocery bags right in front of him—too close in front of him. He had no time to stop.

"Oomph!" Murray, Oliver, and the groceries landed on the ground with a thud.

Oliver looked at Murray. "Are you all right?" he asked. Murray gave a little quack.

Mr. Chips jumped back on the cat wagon and pretended to clean his fur.

"You rat," Oliver whispered. He looked at the mess all around him. A broken egg dribbled down the front of his shirt. Apple juice and milk ran off the curb and into a drain in the street.

Mr. Sanchez and Josh came running out of the store. "What in the world. . . ," said Mr. Sanchez.

"I'm sorry." Oliver apologized to the woman and to Mr. Sanchez. He pointed an accusing finger at Mr. Chips. "I was trying to protect Murray from that cat. I didn't notice anyone leaving the store."

The woman with the ruined groceries didn't look too happy.

"My apologies, Mrs. Willis," said Mr. Sanchez. "I'm sure this young man is prepared to pay for the things he damaged."

"I hope so," said the lady.

Oliver sighed. It hardly seemed fair.

"Felix," said the Cat Lady.

Oliver turned around to see who the Cat Lady was speaking to.

"Yes, Pearl?" replied Mr. Sanchez.

The Cat Lady pulled a tattered cloth purse out of one of her shopping bags. "I'll take care of this," she said. "Naughty Mr. Chips started the whole kit and kaboodle."

"Are you sure?" said Mr. Sanchez.

47

"Quite," replied the Cat Lady.

"I really can pay," Oliver interrupted.

"I wouldn't hear of it," answered the Cat Lady.

"I don't believe it," Josh whispered. "Another lucky thing."

Oliver grinned. "The lucky thing," he whispered back, "was that Murray didn't end up as Mr. Chips' dinner."

CHAPTER
4

Several days later, Oliver, Sam, and Josh sat in the back yard. Beside them were two large boxes of raisins and a weird wood contraption they'd just nailed together.

"This will be the perfect Science Fair project," Oliver explained. "We're going to show how a duck can be trained to do a simple job by conditioned response."

"Conditioned what?" said Sam.

"Conditioned response. It's one way that animals learn things," Oliver explained.

He sat his contraption down. "This board was left over from building Murray's duck house," he said. "Josh and I nailed three doorbell buzzers onto it. The first buzzer goes to a bell, the second to a light, and the third buzzer isn't attached to anything."

"It just looks like a weird board to me," Sam said, shaking her head.

"Well, it's not." Oliver hit one of the three buzzers. "If you ring the first doorbell, a real bell goes off," he said. "But if you hit the second doorbell, it turns on the light. If you hit the third button, nothing happens. We're going to train Murray to ring the real doorbell."

"How?" said Sam.

"We'll do it in steps," said Josh. "First, ring the bell." Sam hit the first buzzer. "Now give Murray a raisin." Murray gobbled the raisin from Sam's hand. Josh smiled. "If we keep this up, Murray will expect a raisin whenever he hears the doorbell."

"This is going to take a lot of raisins," Sam said. "Then what?"

"Step two," Oliver said. "We sprinkle raisins on the right buzzer. Every time Murray eats the raisins, he'll accidentally ring the bell with his bill. Then comes step three: we take away the raisins. But Murray will know that if he hits the buzzer, the bell will ring—and he'll get a raisin. So he'll try every buzzer until he finds the one that makes the bell ring."

Sam smiled. "And we reward him with a raisin, right?"

"Exactly," said Oliver. "Step four. After he hits the buzzers often enough, Murray will eventually learn that only Buzzer One rings the bell. Whenever he sees this setup, he'll go and ring the bell—"

"And that's what they'll see at the Science Fair!" Sam said. "A trained duck!"

"This is the scientific way people train dogs, cats, and birds."

They practiced step one a few more times.

"How long will this take?" asked Sam.

"A long time," said Oliver. "The Science Fair is in one month. To start, we'll practice every day for an hour."

"I have a good idea," said Josh. "Let's keep a record of how long we spend on each step. Then we can print it up on my dad's computer and pass out charts at the Fair."

"Great idea!" Oliver said excitedly. "This is a terrific project. We're sure to win."

By the following Monday, everyone in the school cafeteria was talking about the Science Fair.

"What will your experiment be?" Oliver asked Kim.

"I'm doing something with Hopkins," she answered. Hopkins was her Angora rabbit. "What are you doing?"

"It's a surprise," said Oliver. He smiled at Sam and Josh. "All I can say is that our experiment will star Murray."

Rusty Jackson walked by with an empty tray. "Murray Schmurray," he sneered. "What can you possibly do with that joke of a bird?"

Oliver stood up. "I was waiting for you to say that," he said. The cafeteria grew quiet. "I thought we had a little bet," Oliver continued.

Rusty looked around the room. "You're stupid

enough to bet me?" he said loudly. "You don't even know what my experiment is yet."

Oliver stuck out his hand. "There's no way we're going to lose," he said. "If we do, you can have my stuffed owl."

"Deal," said Rusty. A buzz went through the cafeteria.

"What's everybody staring at?" Rusty demanded. "My experiment is going to be brilliant."

Oliver sat back down.

"Don't worry, Oliver," whispered Josh. "He doesn't stand a chance."

After school, Sam, Oliver, and Josh rushed home to work on their project. When Murray saw them heading toward him with the buzzer board and the raisins, he started to run the other way.

"No, you don't," said Oliver, getting a firm grip on the bird.

"Maybe he doesn't want to practice today," said Sam.

"We don't have time for a day off," Oliver said. He fed Murray a raisin. "Besides, he loves this!"

They sat down to practice. "You go ahead and start without me," said Oliver. "I'm going to let Pom-pom out."

Josh rang the buzzer and fed Murray a raisin. "I hope Oliver knows what he's doing," he said.

"I don't like this," Sam said. "We shouldn't be forcing Murray."

As soon as Pom-pom rushed over, Murray forgot about the experiment and playfully followed Pom-pom across the yard. "Wait!" cried Sam. "Come back here you two."

"Maybe we should try later," said Josh.

"No, " replied Oliver firmly. "This is practice time." He pulled a few raisins out of his pocket. "Here, Murray," he called.

As soon as Murray headed toward the raisins, Pom-pom distracted him. "Stop it, Pom-pom," Oliver called angrily.

"Aw, let them play for a minute," Sam said.

Oliver walked over and picked up Murray. "An experiment is an experiment," he said.

"At least let Pom-pom stay," Sam said.

Pom-pom gave them a pathetic look. Oliver remembered what his mother had told him that night at dinner. "Okay, I guess so," he finally said.

Pom-pom licked Sam's hand.

Josh wrote in his notebook. "Step Number One: Murray would rather play with Pom-pom than ring bells. Oliver says we have to be strict."

After an hour of practice time, both Murray and Pom-pom expected a raisin whenever the bell rang. "We can't afford to feed them both," Josh said.

"You're right," said Oliver. "From now on Pom-pom will have to stay in the house while we practice."

Pom-pom looked at Oliver and started to whine.

"No, you don't," said Oliver. "This time I mean business."

By the week's end, Murray had already reached step two. "We're making good progress," Josh wrote in his notebook.

On Friday, Ms. Callahan passed around a sheet of paper for students to sign up for the Science Fair. "Oliver," she asked, "are you planning to use Murray?"

"Yes," he replied. "Our experiment is a secret though."

Ms. Callahan smiled. "Fine," she said. "We're all looking forward to seeing it."

Matthew came over to play after his karate class on Saturday. It was a dark, rainy day.

"Everyone's dying to know what you're doing with Murray," Matthew said.

"I'll show you, but you've got to promise not to tell." Oliver grinned.

"Right," Matthew replied. "Jennifer thinks you're teaching him to dance."

Oliver showed Matthew the buzzer board and explained how it worked. Since it was so rainy out, they spent most of the afternoon playing games and watching TV.

Around five o'clock, Oliver stood up and stretched. "I think I'll go check on Murray," he said. "Want to come?"

Matthew nodded.

Outside, a steady drizzle fell. Oliver peered through the fog. "I don't see him," he said.

Pom-pom ran between Oliver's legs and out

the back door. On the other side of the yard, he stopped and whimpered.

"Here, Pom-pom," Oliver called. "You're going to get wet." Pom-pom whimpered again. "I guess I'd better go get him," he said to Matthew.

There was a loud crash.

"Ouch!" yelled a voice.

"There's someone by the duck house," Oliver said. He ran to the other side of the yard, then stopped short.

"Rusty!" he shouted. "What are you doing here?"

Rusty stood with one leg inside the overturned duck house. Bits of straw and duck feathers clung to his hair. Standing beside him was his friend Jay Goodman. Murray paced angrily in front of the two boys. Every time one of them tried to move, Murray would hiss ferociously.

"Get your duck out of here," Rusty snarled.

"What are you doing in my back yard?" Oliver demanded.

"Taking a short cut," said Jay. "But your duck started to chase us."

Matthew tugged on Oliver's sleeve. "There's no short cut through here," he whispered.

"Don't you think I know that?" Oliver whispered back.

Jay tried to take a step forward, but Murray grabbed his pants leg. "Ow!" he cried. "He's pinching me."

"You were bothering Murray, weren't you?" said Oliver.

"That's ridiculous," Rusty replied. "We were on our way to see a friend."

Jay let out a howl. "Oliver, get your duck off me!" he shouted.

"Not until you tell us what you were doing," Oliver said.

Rusty gave Jay a dirty look. "You'd better keep quiet," he said.

Jay shook his pants leg. "But he's hurting me," he cried.

"So?" said Rusty.

Jay glared at Rusty. "You and your stupid ideas," he said. "I don't see why this duck is such a big deal. You said if we fed him a few bread crumbs, he'd start to dance." He rubbed his leg. "All this duck can do is bite."

Oliver went over and gently got Murray away. "Serves you right for spying on him," he said. "Now get out of here."

Rusty pulled his leg out of the duck house. "We were going anyway," he growled. "Besides, that duck is too stupid to learn anything. My experiment is going to beat everyone."

As the two boys walked away, Murray hissed angrily.

"That's telling them," Oliver said. He held on to Murray tightly. "They didn't hurt you, did they?" he asked. Murray gave a low, contented quack.

"Good," said Oliver. He gently petted Murray's head. "Good duck."

*   *   *

That night in bed, Oliver tossed and turned. What if Rusty and Jay had hurt Murray? What if Murray had gotten a bread crumb stuck in his throat and couldn't breathe? What if Rusty and Jay had forgotten to latch the gate?

Oliver quietly slipped on his sneakers and tiptoed downstairs. "Murray," he called softly out the back door. He heard a muffled reply.

"Are you okay?" Oliver whispered. He crept over to the duck house and peered in. Murray blinked his eyes.

Oliver gently picked up the duck and carried him back upstairs. He made a nice, soft nest at the foot of his bed and placed Murray in the middle of it. "Just for tonight," he whispered. Murray blinked a second time and then closed his eyes.

Oliver crawled under the covers and pulled up his knees so that he wouldn't disturb Murray's nest. It was important that Murray get a good night's rest. Oliver rolled over and adjusted his pillow. "No problem," he mumbled. Soon they were both sound asleep.

CHAPTER
5

The next morning, Oliver woke to his mother's voice. "Oliver, what is Murray doing in your bed?" she demanded.

Oliver shook his head and looked at the alarm clock. How could he have overslept?

"Sorry, Mom," he said sheepishly. "We had a bad rainstorm last night."

"But he's a duck," said Mrs. Moffitt. "Ducks belong in the water, not in the bedroom."

"I'll take him back outside right away," Oliver said.

Mrs. Moffitt smiled. "Thank you, " she said. Mrs. Moffitt patted Murray's head. "He's a nice pet, isn't he?"

Oliver beamed. He was glad his mother liked Murray so much.

Sam was standing in the back yard. "Thank

goodness," she said. "I thought Murray had escaped."

"He stayed with me last night," Oliver said. He explained how Rusty and Jay had bothered Murray.

"Sounds like Murray would be a good watch duck," Sam said.

Oliver nodded. "He's the best pet I've ever had." He looked at Sam for a moment. "I've been thinking," he said slowly. "Murray is easy to take care of, and I think he's happy here. Once his wing has healed and the Science Fair is over, I want to keep him."

"As a pet?" Sam said. She stared at Oliver. "But he's a wild bird."

"He likes it here," Oliver persisted. "He has everything he needs."

"But he's not yours to keep." Sam was beginning to get upset.

"He is, too," Oliver replied. "Finders keepers."

"Keeping a wild duck is illegal," Sam said.

"He's not wild anymore," Oliver answered. "He's my pet now."

"What do you mean, 'your pet'?" Sam's voice went up. "I found him too, you know. I've taken care of him just as much as you have."

"But you don't want to keep him," said Oliver.

"You can't do this, Oliver," Sam said. "He's not ours. Remember? We promised to return him to the duck pond."

"I've changed my mind," Oliver replied. He walked over to the garage to get the buzzer board. "It's time to practice now," he said.

"Since when did you become the boss around here?" Sam sounded furious.

Oliver spun around angrily. "Murray *wants* to stay here!" he shouted. "Quit being stupid."

"You're the one who's being stupid," Sam said. "All you're thinking of is yourself. You don't really care what Murray wants. You just want to win the Science Fair."

"I've made up my mind. If you don't like it, leave," Oliver said.

"Don't worry," Sam shouted. "I am. And by the way, I quit your stupid project, too."

"Good!" Oliver shouted back. "Who needs you anyway? Get out of my yard. You're trespassing."

Sam stormed off.

Murray looked from her to Oliver and shook his tail. "No problem, Murray," said Oliver. "You're staying here."

A few minutes later Josh showed up. "Where's Sam?" he asked.

"She quit," Oliver replied. "We had a fight because I told her I've decided to keep Murray."

"You have?" said Josh.

"And if you don't like it, you can quit, too!" Oliver said angrily.

"Who said anything about quitting?" Josh said. "Our project is sure to be a winner."

The next day in school, Ms. Callahan told Oliver she wanted to speak to him during recess.

"I understand Sam isn't going to be working on your project anymore," said Ms. Callahan.

Oliver nodded. "That's right."

"Is there a problem?" asked Ms. Callahan.

"No problem," said Oliver. "It's just that we can't agree about a couple of things."

After Oliver left the classroom, Jennifer came running over. "Why didn't you and Sam come to school together? And why aren't you talking to each other?" she asked.

"None of your business!" said Oliver. "Why doesn't everyone just leave me alone?" He walked off angrily.

The rest of the week, Oliver and Josh practiced by themselves for the Fair. Murray was already up to step three. "No stopping us now," Josh wrote in his notebook.

"How's your science project going?" Mrs. Moffitt asked one night after dinner.

"Great," Oliver replied. He carefully rinsed a dinner plate and placed it in the dishwasher.

"It's been a long time since you've taken on any new business," Mrs. Moffitt observed.

"We've been really busy with Murray," said Oliver.

"I haven't noticed Sam around this week," Mrs. Moffitt added.

"She's decided to do another project," Oliver said. He quickly finished rinsing the rest of the dishes.

"Did you two have an argument?" she asked.

"Not really," Oliver replied. He looked at the kitchen clock. "I've got to go, Mom," he said. "I have an amazing amount of homework tonight."

Oliver rushed up the stairs before his mother could ask more questions.

That Friday, Oliver and Murray paid another visit to the Animal Emergency Center. Murray sat calmly with Oliver in the waiting room.

"Hello, Oliver," said Dr. Johnson. "How's our patient doing?"

"Fine," said Oliver. "I think his wing is completely healed."

Dr. Johnson picked up the bird and examined him. "You're right," he said. "We can take the pin out today." He smiled at Murray. "You'll be back at the duck pond in no time, won't you, little fella?"

Oliver swallowed hard. "Right," he said. "As soon as the Science Fair is over." Oliver explained his project to Dr. Johnson.

"Sounds like you have a winning idea," said the doctor. "When is the Fair?"

"Next Friday," Oliver replied

"Good," said Dr. Johnson. "You don't want to keep this bird too much longer, or he'll get too tame to return to the wild."

"No problem," Oliver said. He tried not to look into Dr. Johnson's eyes.

Removing the pin took only a few minutes. Then Dr. Johnson was back with Murray.

"Thanks for your help, Doctor," Oliver said. He handed Dr. Johnson one of his business cards.

Dr. Johnson smiled. "Good luck at the Fair," he said. "You've done a good job with that duck."

Oliver quickly walked outside. The sun shone brightly. "I'm glad that's over with," Oliver said.

"Oliver!"

Oliver turned around and saw Dr. Johnson walking quickly after him.

"Is everything all right?" Oliver asked.

"I just had a thought," said Dr. Johnson. "I have a patient who's looking for someone to walk his two Dalmatians three afternoons a week." He handed Oliver a piece of paper with a phone number on it. "Why don't you give him a call?"

Oliver took the piece of paper. "Thanks, Doctor," he said. He watched Dr. Johnson walk away, then stuffed the paper into his pocket. "I'm too busy right now to watch two Dalmatians," he told Murray. "Besides, we have to make sure you're ready for the Science Fair."

When they reached the corner, Oliver turned left to go home. Murray tugged the other way on his leash.

"No, Murray, this way," said Oliver.

Murray pulled again.

"Okay," Oliver sighed. "Have it your way."

Murray picked up some speed. "Where are you taking me?" Oliver asked. They made another right turn. Arrowhead Park was straight ahead. "Ah-ha!" said Oliver. "We're going to visit your friends."

The edges of the duck pond looked empty today. Oliver didn't see any children at all. Murray was practically running now.

"Slow down," Oliver said. They reached the water's edge.

Murray quacked loudly. He and Oliver were immediately surrounded by a large group of ducks.

"Hello, everyone," Oliver said. He held the leash tightly.

The cluster of ducks moved into the water.

"No swimming today, Murray," Oliver said. "Time for us to go practice for the Science Fair."

Murray sat down.

"Don't you start in, too," Oliver said. He picked Murray up. "You've got a nice pond of your own to swim in back at the house. Anyway, it's too muddy down here."

As Oliver turned to walk away, Murray flapped his wings in Oliver's face. Oliver slipped on a patch of mud and let go of the leash.

Murray flew onto the pond. "Come back here," Oliver called. He looked down at his clothes. "Yuck. Murray, get back this minute."

Murray dunked his head under the water.

"Do you hear me? I'm not kidding," Oliver said.

Murray swam farther out.

Oliver looked to see if anyone was coming. "You asked for it," he said. He took off his shoes and socks and rolled up his pants legs.

Murray was busy cleaning his feathers.

Oliver waded out till the water was up to his knees. "Gotcha!" he said, grabbing the leash.

"Young man," said a voice, "just what do you think you're doing?"

Oliver turned around to find a policeman standing beside his shoes. "Oh, uh, officer," he said, trying to smile. "It's all right." He waved Murray's leash. "This is my pet. I got him for an Easter present."

"You'd better get out of there fast if you don't want a fine," said the policeman.

"Right," said Oliver. He tugged on Murray's leash. Murray squawked loudly. "Enough," said Oliver. He grabbed the bird in his arms. "Are you trying to get me in trouble?" he whispered.

"Yoo-hoo, Oliver. What are you doing in there?"

Oliver's heart sank as he recognized the voices. "Hi, Jennifer. Hi, Kim," he said, trying to sound cheerful.

"People aren't allowed in the duck pond," Jennifer said.

Oliver pretended not to hear her. His feet squished on the bottom of the pond. The mud felt really disgusting. He took two fast steps.

"Stop wiggling," Oliver whispered to Murray.

Oliver had a hard time standing straight.

The policeman walked to the edge of the pond. "Hurry up, young man," he said.

Oliver felt himself slipping. "Not again!" he thought. He and Murray landed with a splash. The other ducks scattered.

Oliver looked up at Jennifer and Kim. They were laughing so hard they were bent over.

"What's so funny?" Oliver said. He grabbed Murray and stomped out of the duck pond. A piece of green slime hung from his ear.

"Wait till they hear about this at school," Jennifer hooted.

Oliver looked down at Murray. "I thought you were supposed to be a lucky duck," he said. "Come on. Let's go home."

CHAPTER
6

Thursday was the day before the Science Fair. Everyone spent the afternoon setting up their exhibits.

"Be careful," Oliver was saying. "We don't want to drop it."

He and Josh were carrying their buzzer board into the cafeteria. It was covered with a large sheet.

"What's *that* supposed to be?" hooted an older student.

"You'll find out tomorrow," Josh said.

"Our table is over there," Oliver said. He stopped suddenly. "Oh, no. Look who has the booth next to us."

Sam was busily bent over her project. "Hello," she said coldly. It looked like steam was rising in front of her.

"What's that?" asked Josh.

"It's dry ice in water," said Sam. "I built a model of a volcano. The dry ice sits inside and looks like volcanic steam."

"That's neat," said Josh.

Sam looked at Oliver. "How's your experiment coming?" she asked.

"It's a big success," Oliver replied.

"Are you still going to keep Murray?" she asked.

"Yes," said Oliver.

Sam shook her head and went back to her project.

"Hi, guys," said Matthew. He was carrying a mobile of the planets. "You going to practice here with Murray today?"

"As soon as we get everything wired up," replied Josh. "I've got a better way to wire all the buzzers." He took out a screwdriver and fiddled for a long time. "That should do it," he said finally. He covered the boards with the sheet again. "Let's go get Murray."

When they got back, almost everyone had set up their booths.

Oliver noticed all the older students over in the far corner. "Let's just do one or two practice tries," he whispered to Josh. "I don't want anyone spying on us."

Oliver sat Murray on the table. Then he raised the sheet so Murray could see the buzzers. "Ring the bell, Murray," he said.

Murray walked over to the right button and hit it with his bill.

"Hey," said Oliver. "No bell. Nothing happened."

"Uh-oh," said Josh. "I'd better fix it."

Murray squawked, and pulled on Oliver's sleeve. Oliver fed him a raisin. "Good duck," he said. "You were right."

"It'll take a few minutes to rewire this," Josh said.

Oliver put Murray back on the floor. "Let's hurry," he said.

"Where's my screwdriver?" Josh asked.

Oliver got so busy helping Josh that he forgot to keep his eye on Murray. Then he heard a familiar hissing.

Josh looked at Oliver. "Uh-oh," he said.

"I can't believe this!" someone screamed.

Oliver rolled his eyes. "I'd know that voice anywhere," he said.

Over in the corner where the older kids had set up their projects, Murray had Rusty backed up against a wall.

"Look what that duck just did!" Rusty yelled.

Oliver stared in disbelief. "Murray!" he said.

Underneath a sign reading TYPES OF BREAD MOLD was a row of empty plates. A moldy crust of bread hung out of Murray's bill.

Rusty pointed an accusing finger at Murray. "He just ate my project!" he said. "I had four different kinds of bread mold growing. Now I have only one!"

Murray swallowed the bread crust.

"None!" said Rusty.

"*That* was your experiment?" said Oliver. "*Mold?*"

"Gross," said Matthew. Jennifer pretended she was going to throw up.

A couple of older kids started to laugh.

Rusty glared. "It's not funny," he said. "I worked a long time on this."

"What about my bird?" said Oliver. "He's lucky he wasn't poisoned. Your moldy bread might have killed him."

Now the whole cafeteria was laughing.

"*I'll* kill him!" Rusty said. He tried to lunge at the duck, but Murray hissed at him.

"Stay away," Oliver warned. "He's dangerous if you get him mad."

Mr. Thompson, the school principal, walked in. "What's going on here?" he asked.

"That stupid duck just ate my project," Rusty sputtered.

Mr. Thompson raised his eyebrows. "All of it?" he said.

Josh was laughing so hard he had to sit down and hold his stomach.

Mr. Thompson walked over and examined the evidence. He bent over and picked up a little piece of moldy bread from the floor. "It looks like you've still got enough for a project here," he said. "I wouldn't worry about it." He walked back into the hall.

"Sorry, Rusty," said Oliver with a grin. "I guess that stuffed owl stays at my house."

Rusty put his head between his hands. "All my hard work," he groaned. "It's not fair."

Sam wandered over to Rusty. "Sorry about your project," she said.

"Why should you care?" Rusty growled.

"It was a good idea," Sam said. She looked right at Oliver. "Too bad some people just care about winning."

Oliver could smell tacos as soon as he walked into his house.

"Mmmm!" he said, bursting into the kitchen.

"There you are!" Mrs. Moffitt smiled. "I wondered if you were ever coming home."

"We stayed late to set up our Science Fair project," Oliver said. "Tomorrow's the big day."

"I know," said Mrs. Moffitt. "You haven't talked about anything else in weeks. How's it going?"

"Fine," Oliver replied. He snitched a bite of grated cheese. "We'll probably win."

"You sound pretty confident," Mrs. Moffitt said.

"It's just that we have a really good project," Oliver said. He got the plates and silverware out.

"What do you hear from Sam?" asked Mrs. Moffitt.

"She's okay," Oliver said. "She's doing something on volcanoes for the Fair." He disappeared into the dining room.

"I thought the two of you were sharing Murray," Mrs. Moffitt called from the kitchen.

"Not anymore," Oliver answered. "When she

quit our project, she quit Murray." He took a deep breath and walked back into the kitchen.

"Mom," he said, "what do you think of Murray?"

Mrs. Moffitt stopped slicing tomatoes. "What do you mean?" she said.

"Do you like him?" Oliver asked.

"Of course," said Mrs. Moffitt. "He's been a very nice house guest."

"What would happen if Murray decided *not* to go back to the duck pond?" Oliver said.

Mrs. Moffitt laughed. "I'm sure he'll be delighted to be back with his friends again. Why?"

Oliver didn't say anything more. Maybe he should wait to tell his mother until after Murray won the Science Fair. He poured two glasses of juice and took them to the table.

"No reason," he called over his shoulder. "I was just hoping you liked him," he said.

Oliver was up early the next morning. He tiptoed to the refrigerator to fix Murray's breakfast.

Oliver pulled a bag of apples and some onions out of the refrigerator. He chopped them all up and then added a little lettuce. He wanted Murray to feel his best today.

"Murray!" he called softly. "Breakfast!" He stuck his head out the back door and looked around.

"That's funny," he thought. "I don't see him."

He walked over to Murray's house. "Rise and shine!" he said.

The duck house was empty.

Oliver started running around the back yard. Then he stopped when he saw the gate in the fence. It was wide open.

"Murray!" Oliver yelled. "Where are you?"

There was no answer.

Oliver ran out the gate and looked up and down the street. Murray was nowhere to be seen.

Oliver's heart pounded. His throat felt dry.

"Murray!" he called again.

All sorts of thoughts started to spin around in his head. How could this happen? Who would want to let Murray out of his pen?

Oliver saw Sam walk out of her house.

"Morning," she said with a wave.

Oliver ran up to her. "Where is he?" he shouted.

Sam frowned. "Who?"

"Murray!" Oliver replied. He wildly looked around Sam's yard. "What did you do with him?"

"What are you talking about?" said Sam.

"Somebody let Murray out through the gate in my back yard," he answered. "And I think you know who did it."

"You're crazy," Sam replied. "I would never do that."

Oliver's heart raced even faster. "Then who let him out, huh?"

"Leave me alone, Oliver," Sam said angrily.

79

"Wait," cried Oliver. "I know who did it. It was Rusty, right? He wanted to get even, so he snuck over here and opened the gate. I bet you even helped him."

"You're out of your tree," Sam said.

"I saw you being nice to Rusty yesterday," Oliver said.

Sam's face went tight. "He had a good project, and I told him so," she said. "What's wrong with that?"

"You two got together and planned the whole thing," Oliver said. "Just to get even with me!"

"I had nothing to do with Murray's escape, and I bet Rusty didn't either," Sam shouted.

"Who stole him then?" Oliver shouted back.

"Did it ever occur to you that maybe Murray left on his own?" Sam replied.

"Murray would never do that," Oliver said. "He *likes* it with me. Besides, he knows today is the Science Fair." Oliver's arms dropped hopelessly to his sides. "It's all ruined," he said. "My pet is gone and my science project is wrecked!" He ran back to his house and slammed the door.

Oliver hardly spoke to anyone all morning. No one except Josh knew about Murray's disappearance. Oliver tried to think of a way to tell his classmates, but whenever he thought about Murray he'd start to get a lump in his throat.

During morning recess, Josh came over.

"Maybe we can try looking for him," Josh said.

Oliver wasn't listening. "He was the best pet

80

I ever had," he said softly. "I still can't believe he's gone."

Josh shook his head. "Do you really think Sam or Rusty let him out?" he asked.

Oliver turned away angrily. "What am I going to tell people?" he said. "What's going to happen at the Science Fair? Everything is ruined." He ran back to the classroom.

"Oliver, wait!" Josh called.

The class was still outside for recess. Oliver put his head down on his desk and tried to think.

He remembered bringing Murray home from school late. He had been the one who shut the gate. Had he been as careful as he could have been?

"Are you all right?" asked Ms. Callahan.

Oliver looked up. "May I be excused during lunch today?" he said. "I lost part of my Science Fair project, and I need to go look for it."

CHAPTER
7

Oliver left school at noon. "Maybe Murray is waiting for me at home," Oliver told himself. The gate to the back yard was still open.

"Here, Murray," Oliver called.

There was no answer. Oliver unlocked the kitchen door to let Pom-pom run around the yard for a minute. Pom-pom dashed over to Murray's house. When he didn't find him, he started to sniff around the yard.

"No, Pom-pom," Oliver said sadly. "Your friend isn't here anymore."

Oliver poked his head inside the Quick Shoppe next. "Hi, Mr. Sanchez," he called. "Have you noticed my pet duck around today?"

Mr. Sanchez shook his head. "Sorry, son," he said.

Oliver bought himself a candy bar and sat on

the curb. He tried to think. Where else could a duck be found?

"Hello, young man."

It was the Cat Lady. She was pulling the same red wagon full of cats.

"Why aren't you in school?" she asked.

"I got special permission to come home for lunch," Oliver said.

The Cat Lady looked around the parking lot. "This is home?" she said.

Oliver looked at his watch. He had to be back in twenty minutes.

"Where's that duck of yours?" she asked.

Oliver was hoping she wouldn't notice. "I'm not sure," he said. Then he remembered how the Cat Lady had helped him look for Jennifer's cat. "Have you seen him?"

She shook her head. "Only place I ever see ducks is at the duck pond. Why don't you try looking there?"

Oliver smiled for the first time all day. "Thanks," he said. "I think I will."

Five minutes later Oliver hurried into Arrowhead Park. He turned left at the duck pond and carefully made his way to the water's edge.

Oliver spotted him in the middle of a large group of ducks.

"Murray!" Oliver shouted excitedly. "You're here! What luck!"

The ducks swam closer.

"I was afraid you ran away," Oliver said. "I'm so happy to find you. Let's hurry. It's almost time for the Fair to start."

The ducks turned and swam away.

"Wait!" cried Oliver. "Where are you going?"

Murray slowed down to look at Oliver.

"It's time to go," Oliver said.

Murray quacked and paddled off to be with his friends.

Oliver's heart started to pound again. "Please, Murray," he begged. "Don't you care about the Science Fair?" Murray was too far out in the pond for Oliver to reach.

Oliver walked to a bench. He sat very still, hoping Murray would forget about him and swim a little closer.

Murray stayed away.

As Oliver watched Murray splash with the other ducks, he thought about what Sam had said: "Murray is a wild bird. He should be free. All you care about is yourself."

"Maybe I *was* being unfair to Murray," Oliver mumbled. "He likes it here. He has lots of friends—and lots more room."

Oliver had enjoyed all the attention he'd gotten when he was with Murray. And all the lucky things. But did he ever think about what Murray wanted? Or what was best for Murray? Winning the Science Fair was important to *Oliver*, not to Murray. Maybe Murray was happiest right here.

Oliver stood up and slowly walked back to the path. He looked back over at the duck pond.

"It's okay, Murray," he said. "I understand."

It was a long walk back to school. Oliver found all the kids lining up outside the cafeteria for

CAFETERIA

SCIENCE
FAIR ←

the Science Fair. "I know I did the right thing," Oliver told himself. "Murray is where he belongs. But how will I explain it to everyone?"

Several students at the end of the line began to laugh and point at Oliver.

"They're laughing at me," Oliver thought. "I guess everybody knows Murray is gone."

"Look who joined the line!" one boy said.

"It's Murray! Yay!" said a girl.

"What?" Oliver said. He turned around.

A white duck stood right behind him. He quacked and waggled his tail.

"Murray!" Oliver shouted. He picked up the duck. Murray must have followed him all the way from the park. Oliver had felt so bad, he'd never looked back. "Thank you, Murray," Oliver whispered. "I know you did this for me."

The whole school filed into the cafeteria. Oliver went to his booth. Josh was already waiting there.

"Where did *he* come from?" Josh whispered.

Oliver patted Murray's head and smiled. "I found him at the duck pond," he said.

Josh looked around the cafeteria. "Well, I sure am glad he's back," he said. "Do you know who the judge is this year?"

"I heard it was someone from outside school," Oliver replied.

Mr. Thompson got on the loudspeaker system. "Attention, boys and girls," he said. "Our judge has just arrived. Before she starts to come around to the booths, I'd just like to introduce her. Some of you may already know Lieutenant

87

Miller from the Fifth Precinct. Please give her a big welcome."

Oliver clapped loudly. "What luck!" he said. "She was the one at the police station when we turned in the watch."

Lieutenant Miller and Mr. Thompson began to work their way around the room.

"There are lots of good exhibits this year," said Josh. "But I think ours is still the best. Good thing Murray showed up."

Lieutenant Miller and Mr. Thompson were looking at Matthew's model of the solar system. "I made the planets out of Styrofoam so they'd be light enough to hang from a mobile," Matthew explained.

Lieutenant Miller looked at Kim's exhibit next. She was pulling tufts of fur right off the back of her Angora rabbit, Hopkins, and spinning them into one long strand of yarn.

"After I spin the yarn," Kim said, "I use it to knit these hats." She held one up. "Angora rabbits shed about four times a year and give up to twelve ounces of wool. People have been using Angora wool since about 1850."

Oliver nudged Josh. "That's really good," he said.

Sam's turn was next. She talked about how volcanoes are formed and explained how she built her volcano out of papier mâché and chicken wire. Everybody liked the dry-ice "steam."

Lieutenant Miller moved on to Josh and Oliver.

"Here's an interesting project," said Mr. Thompson.

Lieutenant Miller looked at Oliver. "Don't I know you?" she asked.

"We found a gold watch in Arrowhead Park and turned it in to you," Oliver said.

The police lieutenant smiled. "Now I remember," she said. "So what have you got here?"

"This is a buzzer board," Oliver said, holding it up. Everyone crowded around for a better look.

"The first buzzer rings a bell, the second buzzer turns on a light, and the third buzzer doesn't do anything." He pointed to Murray, who sat quietly on the table. "Through conditioned response we taught my pet duck, Murray, how to ring the first buzzer."

"Amazing," said Mr. Thompson.

"I thought he was going to dance," Oliver heard Jennifer whispering.

Josh picked up a long computer print-out. "I took notes every step of the way and printed them out here. We divided Murray's learning job into four steps." Josh explained the steps and read off some of the notes he made.

"Day One: Murray finally understands. When we ring the bell he gets a raisin. Now if we ring the bell and don't reward him, he starts looking around for a raisin. He even went over and pulled on Oliver's pocket, where we keep them.

"Day Eight: We stopped early. Murray only wanted to play with Pom-pom." Josh looked up

for a moment. "That's Oliver's dog," he explained.

"Day Sixteen: We tried the experiment using apples instead of raisins. No good."

When Josh finished reading, Oliver spoke. "And now, ladies and gentlemen, please watch." His classmates crowded closer.

"Murray, ring the bell," Oliver said. Murray waddled over and hit the right buzzer. The bell rang loudly. The audience clapped and cheered.

Lieutenant Miller smiled. "Very nicely done," she said. Oliver demonstrated a few more times in case anyone missed it.

Lieutenant Miller moved on around the room. When she got to Rusty's experiment, she studied it for a very long time. "Did the mold eat up all the other pieces of bread?" she asked.

Several students started to snicker until Mr. Thompson gave them a look.

"No, Lieutenant," said Rusty. "I had five types of bread mold growing, but Oliver Moffitt's duck ate them all."

"I'm sorry to hear that," said Lieutenant Miller, looking back at Oliver and Josh.

Rusty began carefully explaining about all of his different kinds of bread mold.

"Why doesn't he shut up?" Josh said nervously. "Did you see the way he tried to get us into trouble?"

"It *was* a pretty good project, Josh," said Oliver.

At last it was time to announce the winner. Mr. Thompson stood at the front of the cafeteria.

"We've had a lot of wonderful exhibits this year," he said. "Bartlett Woods School should be proud of all the hard work its students did. Picking a winner is never easy. I think, though, that most of you will agree that the prize this year should go to Oliver Moffitt and Josh Burns."

A loud cheer went up.

"We did it!" Oliver shouted. "Lucky Murray won the prize!" He and Josh hugged each other and jumped up and down.

Rusty paced back and forth angrily in the corner.

"No fair!" he suddenly blurted out. "My experiment should have won. But that stupid duck ate all my best molds!"

Mr. Thompson grabbed Rusty by the elbow and pulled him out into the hall. A few minutes later, they came back inside.

"Sorry," Rusty muttered.

One of the teachers handed Mr. Thompson the prize. "Since Oliver won our Fair last year, he may want to let Josh keep this year's prize at his house." The prize was an excellent microscope—the kind used in the Science Room.

"Wow!" said Josh. "We'll take turns with it, okay?"

Oliver nodded happily.

Sam shook Oliver's hand. "Congratulations," she said. "I hope you're happy."

"Sam," said Oliver, "I need to talk to you."

"What do you want?" she said.

"I'm sorry I blamed you for letting Murray go.

You would never have done anything to hurt Murray."

Sam didn't say anything.

Oliver took a deep breath and continued. "I've also been thinking a lot about the other things you said. How Murray should be free, and how we should keep our promises. Today I saw that Murray is really happiest at the duck pond. I hate to see him go, but that's his real home."

Sam smiled.

"I'm taking him back after the Science Fair," Oliver said. "Would you like to come with me?"

"Okay," Sam said.

Oliver, Sam, and Murray walked slowly through the park. When they got near the duck pond, Oliver unhooked the leash and Murray took off with a lot of quacking and flapping.

"I'm really going to miss him," Oliver said. Murray had already swum to the other side of the pond.

"It's best for him though," Sam said.

"I know," Oliver replied. "Look how happy he is. He's been trying to tell me this for a long time."

They sat for a while on the bench and watched Murray play with the other ducks.

"We can always come back and visit," said Sam.

"Right," said Oliver. "Anytime." He sat quietly for a few more minutes. "Hey!" he said suddenly. "I wonder if gerbils are lucky?"

Sam laughed and tugged on Oliver's sleeve. "Come on," she said. "Let's get quacking."

They both laughed, and stood up to go. "Sam?" Oliver asked. "What's that campfire song you taught me about ducks?"

" 'Be Kind to Your Web-Footed Friends'?"

"That's the one," said Oliver with a smile. They sang all the way home.